# The Three
# C.E.O.
# Checklists

# The Three C.E.O. Checklists

✦

## A Leadership Process that Actually Works

*Ra Broaddus*

iUniverse, Inc.
New York  Lincoln  Shanghai

# The Three C.E.O. Checklists
## A Leadership Process that Actually Works

iUniverse books may be ordered through booksellers or by contacting:

iUniverse
2021 Pine Lake Road, Suite 100
Lincoln, NE 68512
www.iuniverse.com
1-800-Authors (1-800-288-4677)

Because of the dynamic nature of the Internet, any Web addresses or links contained in this book may have changed since publication and may no longer be valid.

ISBN: 978-0-595-47153-9 (pbk)
ISBN: 978-0-595-70954-0 (cloth)
ISBN: 978-0-595-91433-3 (ebk)

Printed in the United States of America

*To Jane, whose advice and support kept this project moving forward; to Ryan, Sean, and Jillian, who carry these leadership lessons through the next generation.*

*And to Jack Ford, whose consistent message is simply his belief in us.*

# Contents

# *Acknowledgments*

To say that I learned effective leadership processes from the people listed below would not give them enough credit. The whole story is that these people let me so deeply into their organizations and their decision-making that I learned as much from them as they did from me.

As an advisor to these C.E.O.s and owners, I learned that there really is a "best way" to run an organization. I saw that the best leaders, in organizations of all different types, still faced very similar challenges, and approached the challenges very effectively using the same basic processes, even when they weren't aware they were following a process.

From that realization, it was a short leap to convert my notes into *The Three C.E.O. Checklists, A leadership process that actually works*. But none of this would have been possible without the leaders who figured out the processes one step at a time:

Lew Chatham, Bill Cate, Art Katz, Patrick Kennedy, Ken Winfield, Tom Olson, David Moorman, Chas Arnold, Kim Moorman, Mike Lipman, Bob Stafford, Kim Daugherty, Gary Jeffers, Ann Thornton, Jim Burke, Mark Abel, R. O. Rushton, Bengt Lager, Luanne Whiting-Lager, Matty Rost, Andrew Hajduk, Ray Larsen, Laura Mikszan, Greg Mikszan, Bruce Kopkin, Mike Melton, Patti Gosch, Kurt Gosch, Jim Gieselman, Michael Randall, Alex Paulson, Jim Musgraves, Sonny Goodwin, Clay Warner, Larry Isaacson, Richard Isaacson, Marc Carson, Katherine Simons, Craig Simons, Michelle Lee, Lil Kloock, David Warren, Pete Van Cleave, Terry Goldman, Rick Barlow, Rex Fortenberry, Kim Jackson, Brian Will, Clyde Ogden, Tim Gafnea, Pepper Schafer, Jeff Harrington, Jennifer Taylor, Lig Quigley, Gail Evans, Karl Lehman, Tim Lennon, Bill Hosken, Maurice Rosenbaum, Larry Stoumen, Edward Carroll, Ginny Tibbetts, Dave Tibbetts, David Ogletree, David Joiner, Billy Hames, Richard Nelson, Chris Nardone, and Ike Broaddus.

# The Three
# C.E.O.
# Checklists

# Lessons Learned

Lesson #1:

*Life is 100% leadership-driven.*
*The good results and the bad results*
*are all a reflection of leadership.*

Everyone acknowledges that "leaders make a difference," and it's true. But the whole truth is a lot less subtle: leaders absolutely *are* the difference. Every single thing in life moves in the right direction, or the wrong direction, because of leadership.

Within an organization, everything gets done—or doesn't get done—because of processes leaders have or have not set in motion. When things run smoothly and consistently, the leader is doing well. When there are problems, leadership is *always* the problem, and the C.E.O. owns full responsibility.

Sometimes you get lucky early in your career, and get to see important lessons right out of the gate. It's rare, but sometimes as a rookie you're on a team with great leadership, so your early experience shows you how important things are done correctly.

Many years ago, as the Navigator of a U.S. Navy ammunition carrier, I was that rookie on a good team, with a great leader, as we prepared for war. Combat zone demands put us under pressure to pass an intense combat readiness inspection on our first try, though this ship had never done that.

We left the harbor that cold morning, steaming through a narrow channel, with shoals to our right, a simulated mine field to our left, and current setting us left toward the mine field. As my fixes showed the effect of that current, I recommended course corrections to the right, and the Captain ordered those changes. Overall, we had the situation under control. Then we rounded the final bend, and the full force of the current hit us—but no one knew that except the inspectors.

Twenty seconds later, my next fix showed us on the edge of the minefield. I yelled to the Captain, "Navigator recommends hard right rudder, all ahead full"—a radical call in any inland channel—but in this case a call that would point us right at the shoals.

Now, stop for a second and imagine yourself in the Captain's position. He's getting input from all departments, not just mine. He has *prepared* for this; he knows the force of the current *could* increase; he knows he has to avoid the minefield and the shoals at all costs; he knows he can trust my team. But he also knows the stakes are huge, all eyes are on him, and my recommendation is radical.

So—what should he have done?

Without question, most C.E.O.s would have quickly responded "What other options do we have?" Or "Let me take a look." Both would have been sensible responses. And both would have put us in the minefield. The Captain, on the other hand, never hesitated. In one smooth sentence he said "Hard right rudder/All ahead full/Navigator get me another fix." And we avoided the minefield, stayed clear of the shoals, and passed inspection on the first try, because—for the first time in that ship's history—we had the right *leadership*.

That leadership lesson is the good news, and the bad news: good news, because there *are* leaders as disciplined and skilled as that captain; bad news, because there are so few of them.

Our single greatest challenge—the reason organizations spend so much time in minefields—is lack of good leadership. The magnitude of that problem is surpassed only by the magnitude of its symptoms, which include everything from financial instability and undue stress, to perpetuation of the problem and a defeated mentality for so many people within those organizations.

Lesson #2:

*There are many reasons why organizations appear "success-*
*ful", temporarily or incrementally,*
*despite less-than-adequate leadership.*
*But the only reason for organizational distress*
*is leadership failure.*
*Businesses, for example, don't have financial problems. They*
*have leadership problems,*
*with financial symptoms.*

My initial contact with C.E.O. peer groups came
through a friend who owned and ran a service company,
and joined a peer group because he felt unable to remedy
the dysfunction within his own organization. He had
grown his business from scratch, knew it wasn't healthy,
and didn't know where to turn for help. So he figured
he'd meet with C.E.O.s he thought were "successful"—those in the group. What he learned came as a
shock. His fellow C.E.O.s welcomed him for the same
reason. They were struggling; they assumed he was "successful"; they wanted his input.

Stories like this are the rule, not the exception. The
single most pervasive problem faced by organizations is
lack of good leadership. That's a broad-brush indict-
ment, but it's been true for a long time. Labor unions,

for example, exist only because generations of leaders treated their people so horribly that employees had to literally fight back. Over the years, media reports of corporate distress haven't changed much. You're always left to wonder how C.E.O.s could have gotten their organizations that far upside-down.

Everyone sees the examples. Who do you know, who thinks the places where they've worked are well organized, with great leaders? Practically no one—and they're right.

"Organizational dysfunction" is considered redundant terminology. Organizations are *assumed* to be dysfunctional, and the culprit is assumed to be either size alone (in larger organizations), or "entrepreneurial spirit" (in smaller ones). But the true culprit is simply lack of good leadership.

As easy as it is to understand leadership, the job itself is hard. But that's the point: It's not for everyone. Leadership requires disciplined, skilled, unselfish people—and average people won't make that effort. C.E.O.s own responsibility for tough choices, and that's a burden you must *want* to bear, to play at the leadership level.

Lesson #3:

*It's up to you.*
*Unless you choose to make your improvement*
*part of the solution,*
*you're part of the problem.*

It wasn't long after the dawn of aviation that the U.S. Navy established itself as the benchmark for pilot skill. And yet, years later, research on the Navy's aviation disasters showed a startling conclusion: a disproportionate number of pilots lost were the Navy's best.

How could this be? How could the best of the best be the ones making more errors? The answer was found in the simplicity of the Navy's solution: *checklists*. Until then, nobody realized that the best pilots still needed checklists for every aspect of their work—preparing their aircraft for takeoff, in-flight transitions, combat maneuvers, emergencies, safe landings—every conceivable evolution in flight. And to this day, a mainstay of aviation is checklists.

The same should be true at the C.E.O. level. The best leaders have found solutions—the right disciplines and skills, organizational structure, and operating processes. What's been missing is the *discipline* to quantify those solutions, put them into checklists, and follow the checklists.

With few positive exceptions—and there are some great exceptions—we still act like we don't know what it takes to develop, coach, and grade leaders. Historically, leadership literature has actually hurt the cause, primarily by fueling the perception that leadership is complicated, and secondarily by drilling down into false conclusions. Many people, for example, have touted "the leader-manager difference" to foster a mystique about "leaders", differentiating them from "managers": i.e. "leaders innovate; managers administer"; "the leader does the right thing, the manager does things right". In reality, there is no line separating leadership and management. Leaders innovate *and* administer; do the right thing *and* do things right; exercise vision *and* hit this year's numbers.

Leadership has been called an "art". Great leadership can *appear* to be an art, but to understand that point, understand the terminology: in human skill-sets, art and science are not separate. Art is simply the mastery of science. Every human action is the result of processes (whether or not we understand those processes), but it can look like art when you've mastered it. I've watched a

Japanese potter decorate his work. With a half-dozen brush strokes in about three seconds, he created something so beautiful it held my attention. What he did in those three seconds was actually a *process*—a series of chemical reactions, nerve impulses, and muscle movements, which, through his mastery, appeared as art. That process could be programmed into a robotic arm to produce identical art.

Such is the case with leadership. It's very much a *process*, based on disciplines and skills. When you've mastered the process, you'll make leadership look like an art.

Lesson #4:

> *Leadership is not simply*
> *the C.E.O.'s most important job.*
> *It's their only job.*

Because leadership is the C.E.O.'s only job, performance at the C.E.O. level is graded solely on three broad measures of organizational health:

- *Consistent profitability.*

- *Stakeholder delight—*
  *(owners, employees, customers, vendors).*

- *Setting and reaching goals.*

Success in those three areas depends on leadership—how diligently the C.E.O. maintains the most effective *organizational structure* and *operating processes*.

Structure and Process are inter-dependent. Within your organization, you have to know what processes are required, what positions are needed to execute those processes, and what measures will tell you that people in those positions are doing a great job.

C.E.O.s frequently assume that one particular strength (i.e. sales, industry knowledge, passion, or even tenure) is needed at their level, and that leadership either follows that strength, or can be hired. That is the single most blinding assumption a leader can make. C.E.O. disciplines and skills are the only strengths needed—because leadership is the C.E.O.'s only job. The three C.E.O. checklists will lay out the steps to do that job.

# Checklist #1
# C.E.O. Disciplines and
# Skills

*In any leadership role, people who burn out
didn't have the discipline to do the job
in the first place.*

At the C.E.O. level, discipline and skill are essentially one. Effective leadership—the world's most challenging job—requires a superior level of skill that can be maintained *only* with strong personal discipline.

Leadership goes beyond title or position—it's a commitment to organizational health. The ability to succeed with that commitment rests on the six disciplines and skills of Checklist #1:

• Health Management.

• Focus.

- Credibility.

- Decisiveness.

- Negotiation.

- Communication.

If you're in a designated leadership role, use Checklist #1 as a personal reference. You'll see where you stand, and where you need to make progress. If you're hiring for leadership positions, use Checklist #1 as a guide for interviews and evaluation.

# Health Management

Managing your health is the primary leadership discipline. No matter what else you think is important in life; you can't get it done without your health.

Leadership requires a very healthy mind, which requires a healthy body. The energy leaders need to consistently maximize their abilities, to stay rational, to maintain focus on organizational health, to process input from diverse sources, to make tough decisions quickly, to follow up, to stay positive, all requires a higher level awareness and *control* of their physical, mental and emotional wellness. The key to that control is a nine-step process:

1. *Professional screening and advice.* Obviously, it starts here. You're the C.E.O. of your life, so health decisions are yours—not your doctor's. But start with regular check-ups and advice from professionals you trust.

2. *Stress reduction.* Understand that stress is life's deal-killer—negatively affecting performance, relationships, mental fitness, immune systems—you name it. The solution, however, is just as powerful: one hundred percent of the stress in your life is stress *you*

*allow.* So it's entirely possible to think through every stressful situation that life throws at you, and take the stress out of it. Make that your rule, and eliminate exceptions.

When you feel overwhelmed, learn to talk through issues with peers/mentors. Rely on schedules, because relying on memory is stressful. Procrastination adds stress, so make decisions quickly. Delegate more. Delegate entire processes, so that fewer action items land back on your desk. Tend to decline invitations. Overall, simplify your life.

3.  *Self-Respect.* An ancient proverb said, "Self-respect is the cornerstone of all virtue." A cornerstone analogy is just as appropriate in leadership, where the discipline to maintain respect for one's own value, dignity, and character is the basis from which leaders can accomplish several things:

    Leaders with self-respect enable others to use their abilities. Without self-respect, leaders don't see those abilities, because their focus is on validating their own ability.

    Self-respect allows leaders to work without recognition, and to learn from their failures through objective assessment. It allows leaders to share the credit when it lands on them, and to share the blame when it lands on their people, all of which delivers a powerful message to their own people and to anyone else involved.

Leaders with self-respect think of other people as peers. They treat people with genuine courtesy, and appreciate their contributions. Good leaders treat the Chairman of the Board and the newest entry-level hire identically.

Self-respect allows C.E.O.s to learn from others, including their direct reports. They're aware that surrounding themselves with people who consistently agree with them is an enormous organizational weakness, actually limiting their own growth. With self-respect, they're able to make themselves essentially the "weak link", surrounding themselves with people they respect, who can teach them something. Effective C.E.O.s are good listeners and good learners. They and their people are well aware that decisions rest with the leader, but it's their self-respect that enables leaders to feel, and clearly communicate, respect for the input of others.

4.  *Humility*. Healthy leaders are humble people, which is key to developing leaders within the organization. Humility allows leaders to set up their peers, direct

reports, and successors for even greater success. Day to day, humility lets leaders attribute success to factors other than themselves. And when things go wrong, humble leaders take full responsibility.

One of the best talks I've heard was given by a "humor consultant", whose clients included hospitals, where clinical research has documented the connection between laughter and physical well-being. Humor, it turns out, has finally gotten the recognition it deserves. Humor is primarily about stress reduction. In leadership situations, the best humor is self-deprecating. Humble leaders take responsibility seriously, but they don't take themselves seriously.

5. *Rest.* A human body simply has no substitute for rest. The lesson is: get to bed early, so you get to sleep early. The key to adequate rest is not your wake-up time—it's the time you get to sleep.

6. *Nutrition.* Based on your age, metabolism, and vital signs, learn what your body needs, including plenty of water. Control your diet accordingly—not by lifestyle or travel schedule or the preferences of others, but by your body's needs.

7. *Positive attitude.* This is not only your best leadership tool; it's the only outcome of the health management

process that's completely within your control. What happens to you in life, and what happens to you on a daily basis, is much less important than the attitude with which you choose to react to it. You have total control over that choice, so choose healthy reactions.

Attitude is one of many ways an organization mirrors its leader. When there is negativity among your people, someone in a leadership role is either modeling or enabling that behavior.

8. *Regular exercise.* There's a level of physical activity that's right for you, and it needs to be part of your routine.

   Beyond exercise, sports research has shed more light on *strength.* Sports psychologists have learned that physically stronger players have better emotional endurance, more sustained focus, and better mental toughness. In other words, a connection has been established between physical strength and mental strength. Since leadership success depends on mental strength, you'd do well to include a strength-training program with your exercise regimen.

9. *Relationships.* Your parents were right: people will judge you by the company you keep. Now that you're an adult, there's more to it: First, both your

emotional health and your success in life are influenced most by the relationships you choose. Second—and this can be a life-changing realization—you totally control those choices. There is not a single person—family member, friend, neighbor, boss, peer—who you are obligated to spend time with. At home, at work, and at play, choose relationships *only* with people who are trustworthy and positive, and who respect your contribution.

# Focus

What makes a cornered animal so dangerous? You may be surprised to hear it explained this way, but the answer is *focus*. As danger approaches, extraneous thoughts are literally filtered out, and total focus is on *closure* to the current issue.

The same concept applies to leadership. Good leaders are detail people, with big-picture perspective. They see the forest *and* the trees, but have the discipline to filter out distractions. Their focus is a single-minded concern for organizational health, doing the things that move the organization forward: building the right relationships, ending the wrong relationships, performing profitably, setting and reaching goals.

At the C.E.O. level, focus has four component disciplines consistently applied:

1. *Time Management.* The key to time management is eliminating things you shouldn't be doing in the first place. Effective C.E.O.s reverse the 80/20 rule, and spend the majority of their time on things that actually improve the organization. They use a *triage* system to determine quickly what is important and what is not. They use a *filter* system to determine

whether something is an opportunity or a distraction, because they know there is no middle ground. Good leaders allow few distractions.

2. *Preparation.* Remember the lesson from high school coaches: "The will to win means nothing without the will to prepare." As true as that is in sports, it's critical in leadership.

   Flight school provided daily illustrations of the discipline of preparation. Student pilots are taught to prepare, but frequently forget how much better prepared are instructors. Every time we were "out-thought" or "out-maneuvered", we found out later we were really "out-prepared". Flight instructors over prepare for classroom sessions and training flights with plans that include strategy, tactics, *and* probable student responses and counter-responses, so that no part of their job is "seat-of-the-pants".

   Critical lesson here for organizational leadership: preparation requires work, but it is literally the only way to fly.

3. *Follow-Up.* U.S. President Ronald Reagan's administration, during their Strategic Arms Reduction Talks with the Soviet Union, gave perhaps the world's most concise argument for follow-up. The Soviet

position on follow-up was simply that they could be "trusted". The U.S. countered—correctly—that follow-up is unrelated to trust, and essentially said, "We *will* trust. And we will verify."

At all levels of leadership, what doesn't get monitored doesn't get done. It has nothing to do with trust, or any possible lack of confidence in your direct reports. It's simply some sort of natural law, which says that organizational results require leaders to follow up.

Effective leaders *proceduralize* their follow-up. Here's the best technique: delegate responsibility for the follow-up at the same time you delegate responsibility for the outcome. In other words, if your direct report is responsible for an outcome in six weeks, and you really need to know their progress weekly, make them responsible for calling you with that weekly report, and for following a specific agenda on that reporting call.

4. *Passion.* Passion is listed last, because without the other disciplines passion is a liability. As important as passion is, it's important *only* when the other disci-

plines are in place, and then it's an essential element of focus.

The right people will get energized about the organization's mission when they see energy modeled and communicated at the leadership level. The same concept applies to performance. The right people will care about doing their best work when they know the leadership cares about them.

Leaders have a much easier time maintaining focus when they maintain *passion* to champion their organization—its values, mission, people, and delivery.

# Credibility

Credible leaders have the discipline to exhibit three consistent behaviors:

1. *Truthfulness.* This is the fundamental, simplest to describe, yet most overlooked behavior. There is no reason to spin truth, or fail to acknowledge that it is what it is. People know it; they expect you to know it; anything short of that shows them you can't be trusted. This is why the term "political leader" has become an oxymoron.

2. *Fairness.* Because people are passionate about fairness, it's a huge component of credibility. This is the behavior they expect from leaders:

   • Treat people with respect. If there is someone on the team you can't respect, remove them from the team.

   • Enforce a non-political environment. Maintain one agenda: what's best for the organization.

   • Don't show favoritism, even when it's politically correct to do so. Credible leaders choose the best people, period.

- Take the heat for organizational errors. Do it quickly and sincerely. Then go back to your people and fix the problem.

3. *Commitments kept.* Credible C.E.O.s do everything they say they'll do. Which shows why credibility is a discipline: tracking your many commitments requires effort, but effective leaders are disciplined to make the effort. As in customer service, a good recovery is better than a perfect delivery. Leaders aren't expected to be perfect. They *are* expected to recover.

   Many years ago, a national news story told of a New England owner/C.E.O. who had committed to not lay off workers despite hard times. Then things got worse. A fire destroyed his facility. He rebuilt, *and* kept his people paid while the facility was being rebuilt. That's extreme, but a great example: He had several reasons not to keep his commitment, but he chose the one reason for keeping it—credibility.

# Decisiveness

The C.E.O.s I work with are some of the most decisive change-managers in business. And yet, in our follow-up "lessons learned" discussions, I hear a consistent theme: they rarely regret their decision, but generally feel they were not decisive *enough*, that their decision should have been made sooner.

Here are three keys to decisiveness:

- Decision-making at every level should be a *consultative* process (other people have input, but the leader makes the decision), not a consensus process where you need agreement.

- A good decision is your best choice; a bad decision is your second-best choice; no decision is your worst choice.

- You rarely have all the information you need. Get all you can, make the call, and follow up. Good leaders take action—quickly. If later information shows you made the wrong call, change it, explain why, and move on.

Inside the mind of a leader, decisiveness is a function of *courage*. Courage has the same definition in leadership as anywhere else: the discipline to act, without fear, in the face of danger, difficulty, or uncertainty.

In leadership, the daily practice of courage is the leader's willingness to hold others to standards. C.E.O.s enforce accountability across the board, using their own mix of rewards and consequences. Because of their courage, and in particular their willingness to enforce *consequences*, they're able to front-end more issues, and allow less drama into their organization.

# Negotiation

Negotiation is the skill we use in so many ways every day. At work and at home, dealing with peers, employees, vendors, customers, children, spouses, and salesmen, we're always negotiating, even in situations where we don't realize it.

At the leadership level, negotiating anything from an employee review to an asset purchase, the process is generally more formal. The C.E.O. approach is win-win, because those deals are the basis for *relationships*. Win-win isn't always possible, but if you follow a process, you'll most likely steer clear of trouble.

At the outset, as soon as you know a negotiation is looming, answer two questions:

1. Is your counterpart competent enough to understand the deal *and* get it done?

2. Can your counterpart be trusted?

If either answer is "no", the negotiation is set up to fail, so the wise decision is to walk away. If both answers are "yes", press on.

Your odds of a great outcome depend on mutual respect and trust. So job #1, which starts before the negotiation and carries through the process, is to earn respect and build trust.

Job #2 is preparation. In any negotiation, the majority of your time and resources should be spent preparing in five areas:

1. Know the numbers behind your goals, priorities, and deadlines. Nail down your position—exactly what you want, what you want *most*, and what you're willing to give up.

2. Know when you'd walk away from the deal.

3. Learn as much as you can about the other side's goals, priorities, and deadlines.

4. Know what laws, rules, contracts, and protocol apply to the situation.

5. Know *whom* you're dealing with. Learn as much as you can about them.

Understanding *priorities* is key to making the deal. Let's say each side wants three things. What's the one thing each side wants most, and how can they get it?

Odds are, that one thing is not the same for each side, so they can get it. But if it is the same, break it down to which aspect is most important to each side, and go from there. Rarely will you have to go head-to-head on a critical point. But if you do, stick to the ten basics of any negotiation:

1.  From the beginning, act like the deal is going to happen. Get the other side to take mental ownership of a deal.

2.  Ensure that you are dealing directly with the other side's *decision-maker*. This is always possible, so push for it.

3.  Get mutual commitment on the agenda and time frame. Then get the other side to disclose their shopping list. Then go as far as possible to have the other side make the first offer.

4.  Your first offer, or counter, should be on the high side of reasonable.

5.  Assuming you've done your homework, there's a good chance you won't have to move from your original number. Make necessary moves in small increments.

6. Patience is critical, as long as the other side stays within the agreed upon time frame. Timing is very important. Greater concessions happen right before deadlines.

7. Stay creative. The best negotiators are good "outside the box" thinkers. Find or create valuable alternatives for each side.

8. Keep the dialog going. And keep it positive.

9. If necessary, force the other side to deal fairly. Protest quickly and firmly if trust or commitment or protocol is violated. Insist that the other side rectify the wrong, and don't give in on that point. When you're dealt with fairly, but caught off-guard, admit your surprise, and buy time to prepare your response.

10. Leave something on the table.

At the C.E.O. level, great negotiators don't make headlines. They don't make enemies, and they don't intimidate people. They make deals pretty quickly, because they're prepared. More importantly, they walk away from a lot of potentially bad deals and troublesome negotiations.

They ask questions, like "What would really be best for you"? They listen "between the lines", and gather information. They learn what's important to people; then they try to give it to them, in exchange for something that's not as important to them. It's an easy skill to practice.

# Communication

In leadership, communication begins with presence, because you can't provide leadership from a distance. Presence gives you visibility, enhances feedback, and ultimately gives your communication credibility.

Great communication requires the discipline to practice four related skills:

- Inter-personal.

- Listening.

- Learning.

- Coaching.

1. *Inter-personal skills* are what you use all day to relate to people. The skills are heavily attitude-based—you must *believe* in the strengths and contributions of the people who work for you. (If you can't believe in them, they shouldn't be on your team.) Communicate your respect and sincerity with positive reinforcement, so you motivate people to want to relate to the organization and to your leadership. People need to perceive that the organization's culture will help them personally. You create (or prevent) those

perceptions through your inter-personal skills on a daily basis.

2. *Listening skills* are your greatest challenge, simply because humans are not wired to listen well. In inter-personal communication, people tend to hear what they want to hear. All of us have filters in our ears, and we filter out communication that challenges our beliefs or feelings or processes or whatever works best for us. So as leaders, where listening skills are critical to our performance, we need the discipline to remove those filters. Tactically, the best listening method is to take notes, because that forces you to focus on what's being said. Short of that, at least make the effort to focus on the speaker, not think about your response, and ask questions to clarify what you think you heard. Listening means creating both the process and the motivation for people to give you quality feedback. It also means understanding what you're hearing.

3. Great leaders have great *learning skills*. They think of themselves not as experts, but as students. They know they're good at what they do, but their achievements have simply shown them how much more they have to learn—and they *want* to learn. Leaders soak up knowledge. Obviously, this is a

wonderful skill for anybody to practice as a key for personal growth, but relative to leadership, there are two enormous tangible benefits:

*Change* becomes your friend. Improvement is critical for the success of any organization, but only learners are comfortable with that. In a leadership position, a major part of your job is managing the change that improvement requires. As a learner, it's a lot easier to front-end that process, to see change while it's still on the horizon, to differentiate good change from bad change, and to make the right decisions.

*Resourcefulness* is easier to coach. Leaders need creative, "out-of-the-box" thinking from their entire team, and that type of thinking comes much more easily to people who want to learn.

4.  *Coaching skills* are the easiest of the four to practice—but you're doomed if you fall into the trap of practicing this one and ignoring the other three. Even in coaching, your job is heavily listening-dependent. Whether rolling out goals or coaching tactical steps for project execution, coaching includes

listening to hear that your message was received, and listening for improvement ideas from others.

Great coaches are simple communicators. In any discussion, they see the essential points, and can explain those points in a way people understand.

For coaching to work, three foundations must be in place: first is an understanding of where the organization is headed. Goals must be known. Second is individual competence: ability, attitude, training, and processes in place. No amount of coaching can make up for an absence of competence. Third is a no-excuses culture. Leaders create that culture, through their coaching, by clearly defining results expectations and focusing on *responsibility for solutions*.

# Checklist #2
## Organizational Structure

People need structure. Humans throughout their history have been "pack animals", relying on "pack" structure for survival and growth. In an organization, leadership effectiveness depends on structure. It's as critical to the health of a startup as it is to an established business. And veteran C.E.O.s misunderstand it as often as entrepreneurs: you really don't need extraordinary people on your team; you need good people—the right people—within the right *structure*.

But what is "structure"? Isn't it just an "org chart"? Well, it's just an org chart if you think a human being is just a skeleton. Structure actually has three elements:

• Higher Goals.

- Values and Culture.

- Positions/Accountability/Reporting.

# Higher Goals

Within an organization, there is one fundamental human dynamic underlying the importance of higher goals: people need to see that the organization is headed somewhere, and that "somewhere" is an even better place. Key to keeping an entire organization energized is the pervasive awareness of those higher goals. Leaders must feel *confident* and communicate confidence in the group's ability to get there.

At the C.E.O. level, two steps will let you articulate your higher goals:

1. Get comfortable with your own personal end game. Take the time to think it through: what you want out of life, how that relates to why you're in business, and what you want your business to accomplish.

2. Visualize the organization at that level of accomplishment: size, basic differentiators, and deliverables. That mature organization and its accomplishments are your higher goals.

# Values and Culture

Inside an organization, people have a collective *cul-ture*—a combination of traits and behavior patterns that describe an organizational identity as clearly as a finger-print. The foundation of that culture is *values* by which people operate every day.

Those values come from our leadership. Cul-ture—positive or negative—exists whether or not the C.E.O. has proactively created it. So it's critical for orga-nizational health that the C.E.O. take the lead in this area:

- *Choose* values wisely.

- *Demonstrate* values.

- *Instill* values throughout the team.

The values choice is proprietary—it's what a leader chooses to live by. Interestingly though, there are five values you see in nearly every healthy organizational cul-ture:

1. *Openness.* In an organization, secrets impede progress. Good people accomplish more when more

information—goals, plans, financial data, results, you name it—is shared.

2. *Truthfulness*. Large issues begin when truth is hidden, distorted, or spun. On the other hand, solutions always present themselves when you and your people consistently confront reality truthfully.

3. *Humility*. It's as essential in an individual's health management process as it is throughout an organization, because humility allows people to respect the contributions of others. That cycle of respect and contributions is what enables a team to be more than a collection of individuals.

4. *Responsiveness*. Culture should reinforce the message, externally and internally, that we *care*. Timely responses, even if we don't have answers, are a powerful start on that message. Conversely, nothing does more to damage credibility than lack of responsiveness.

5. *Responsibility*. Good leaders, and good people in well-run organizations, take responsibility for front-ending what needs to happen, and take responsibility for what doesn't get done. The sooner you own a problem, the sooner good people are willing to help.

The culture you choose (or the culture you allow, if you haven't been proactive) is the foundation for the way your organization operates. Once you've established values, there are three steps to instill and maintain the right culture:

1.  Script the hiring process to screen for values as an initial filter through which candidates must pass.

2.  Script the review process so that people are actually graded on adherence to values.

3.  Walk the talk. No matter what is written or taught, people will know that the organization's values are what the leader demonstrates and tolerates in others.

# Positions/Accountability/Reporting

We're all in the people business. What our organization accomplishes depends on what our people accomplish. But we're an organization—not just a collection of individuals—and on that team people occupy positions. So *before* we assemble the team, we have to know:

• Which *positions* we need.

• What *accountability* each position owns.

• To whom each position *reports*.

   Five fundamentals govern the position chart:

• Based on higher goals, you plan to grow the business to a certain size. Create the chart for *that size*. The chart will include positions not yet filled or not yet full-time.

• Less is more. In organizational hierarchy, flatter is *always* better.

• Leave the humans out of it. Create the positions best for the organization, without regard to strengths and weaknesses of specific individuals. Later, you'll put existing people where there's a fit.

- Understand that nothing about the chart is written in stone. It should be changed whenever change is necessary.

- Always force the chart to work. The right positions and the right people are the C.E.O.'s responsibility. If a C.E.O. ever needs to circumvent the chart by hiring consultants or working on the front line to see what the problems are, the real problem is poor leadership somewhere within the top two levels of the chart.

With those fundamentals in mind, here are three steps to create and update the chart:

1. Look at the *processes* for everything the organization does. If your processes are not yet created, you still know process outcomes: what must be accomplished to deliver your product/service mix to external customers, and support your internal customers?

2. Based on your processes, what front-line positions are needed to produce those results?

3. What leadership/management positions are necessary to provide the level of oversight for *consistent* results, improvement, and leadership development within the organization?

# Checklist #3
## Operating Processes

Every task within an organization is part of a process, whether or not those processes were designed or just grew out of work habits. In well-run organizations, processes are designed, *managed*, and improved.

Processes are designed around *outcomes*, not around tasks or departments. A process has steps, times, and accountable people. It has a clean beginning, includes all tasks relevant to finishing that process, and ends with a product or service for an external or internal customer.

When processes are in place, individual checks and controls are actually reduced, because people are focused on completing a process. Ultimately, there's less organizational drama, because leaders manage processes, and spend less time managing people.

When designing and improving processes, it's critical to manage the role of technology. Despite the fact that most technology-specific functions are delegated, anyone in a leadership position must understand the role technology plays within the organization, and how it affects not just written communication and financial reporting, but every process from strategic planning through service delivery.

There are five types of operating processes:

- Planning.

- Product/Service Delivery.

- Financial Reporting.

- Business Development.

- Human Resource Management.

# Planning

Effective C.E.O.s have learned that planning can never be ignored. With every initiative, inadequate results are almost always traceable to inadequate planning. Four fundamentals help explain why planning is critical to organizational success:

1. Planning lets leaders think through their own buy-in. Before you can lead an organization to accomplish anything, you need to know that it's the *right* thing, and you need to be energized by the process of getting it done. That energy determines the level of focus you can maintain.

2. Planning lets leaders realistically assess the *feasibility* of what they want to accomplish. Articulating and analyzing the actual steps in a plan gives you the best look at what can get done and what can't.

3. Planning gives you the primary tool you need to accomplish what you plan: the checklist of steps for *follow-up*.

4. You can't outsource any of the steps. The entire planning process, from goal setting through follow-up, produces results when done by those who will execute the plan. Good people work harder to reach

plan goals when they know their input led to the plan.

C.E.O.s need three types of plans:

- *Strategic Plans.* Long-range plans to reach the organization's higher goals.

- *Operating Plans.* Tactical plans for current-year results.

- *Succession Plans.* Identify and prepare future leaders; define exit steps for current leaders.

# Strategic Plans

Higher goals define where we're headed long-term. *Strategic* planning is the process of translating those goals into the steps to get there. That process should show us we're headed in the right direction, for the right reasons. In most organizations, strategic planning loses its effectiveness because of the tendency to think, "we're done" when the plan is made. The real key to strategic planning is the follow-up—our ability to follow the *execution checklist*, and revisit the plan every year.

Strategic Plan steps:

1. Look at what the organization does (or will do) to deliver its own unique product/service mix. Within all of that, where are we *outstanding*? What can we do better than anybody else?

2. Within those areas, what *energizes* us?

3. Define a customer base who *needs* that, and is large enough and healthy enough to pay (good margins) for that.

4. Within those areas, and for that customer base, what would we like to accomplish? How would we trans-

late those accomplishments into specific measurable goals?

5.  *Who* owns responsibility for each goal?

6.  *When* should each goal be accomplished?

7.  How will we measure progress?

8.  Write the *execution checklist*: what, when, and to whom the accountable people must report.

## Operating (one-year) Plans

Given your strategic plan, how much can be accomplished this year? That's the basis for your operating
plan—a one-year plan, which is essentially reduced to a
financial projection, or "budget", even though it
includes outcomes that are not measured directly by
Income Statement line items. It's the plan used on a
daily/weekly/monthly basis to know how the organization is doing, and what changes are needed.

The operating plan process itself must be *routine*. At
the same time each year, do the plan for next year; at the
same time each month (or as frequently as necessary),
routinely compare actual to plan, and take whatever
action is needed. This regular comparing and follow-up
is what delivers the message to your people that they
control their numbers.

The more information you share with your people,
and the more input you expect from them in the planning process, the greater your odds of a realistic plan and
positive results.

To that end, many C.E.O.s have built an "open-
book" culture into their organization—teaching their

people *all* the processes of managing a healthy business. They've learned that people who are trusted with more information and more responsibility for organizational success, will expand their roles, and take responsibility for improvements.

Operating Plan steps:

1. *Goals.* What do you want to accomplish for the year? Operating goals should be both achievable and aggressive. Achievable first, because all is lost at the outset if people believe otherwise. But achievable goals should be stretch goals. When people reach beyond their comfort zone, good people do their best work, and bad people leave. Both of those are things you want to happen.

   An operating goal is an *outcome*, not an activity. "Improving customer service", for example, is an activity. "Maintaining 90% customer retention for the year" is an operating goal. The better you can narrow the goal, the better you can plan steps to reach the goal. "Increasing *services* sales by $84,000" is better than "increasing *sales* by $84,000", because the narrower definition lets you focus action where it's needed.

Going back to your strategic plan, what goals should be set for the year? Since the operating plan becomes a financial projection, (with other items), it's best to think it through in the order of an Income Statement:

- Revenue.

- Direct costs of revenue.

- Overhead.

- Other.

2. *Accountability.* Right from the start, get clarity and closure on which individual owns responsibility for each operating goal, and each line item on the Income Statement. Some C.E.O.s put that individual's initials next to each line item description on the Income Statement.

3. *Time Frame.* Operating goals and plans need specific deadlines. A goal is defined as much by its time frame as by any other criteria. "Increasing services sales by $7,000 *a month*" is better than "increasing services sales by $84,000 over the next year" because the shorter time frames increase the likelihood for timely corrective action.

4. *Measures.* You can't manage what you can't measure. All efforts to accomplish your plans depend on how diligently you use the measuring tools for each outcome. If customer service, for example, is an issue, and you develop a plan for improvement, you need an accurate improvement *measure.*

   What financial numbers measure your goals and progress? They become the line items on your Income Statement projection.

5. *Follow-Up.* For people to take ownership of plan results, scorekeeping has got to be *ritual.* At some *regular* time—weekly, monthly, as often as necessary—the team needs to be brought together to review financial results compared to plan. There may be more than one team, perhaps a leadership team which meets first, perhaps departmental or project teams, so long as the reviews reach everyone who can affect results. Changes to the plan can be made at these meetings, because you've got later information. But the point is that you're having these meetings in the first place. You're following up the planning process with continuous information and accountability.

   All operating results, relative to the plan, are fair discussion material. If sales are not what the sales force planned—higher or lower—the sales force has some explaining to do, and the team needs to evaluate the explanation and see if changes are needed. If expenses are not as planned, accountable people need to explain why. If these meetings are held on a regular schedule, and if it's clear that those in charge want to hear the explanations, then people at all levels in the organization will receive the message that they are accountable for their numbers, and will act accordingly.

## Succession Plans

Veteran C.E.O.s have learned that the challenges of starting a business pale in comparison to the challenges of exiting the business on your terms. And it doesn't help the situation that there is so much misinformation on the subject of exit strategy. So, from the perspective of people who have navigated the succession-planning path, here are five largely misunderstood concepts to keep in mind:

- The *leadership transition* is more important than the ownership transition. Whether your primary goal is business continuation or simply a clean exit, the business is more valuable if the right leaders and the right processes are in place.

- The company's *culture* and its *people* are its two most valuable assets.

- The company's ongoing operations must pay for the transition.

- A Management Buyout (MBO) is your first choice, because it carries a higher likelihood of both a fair price *and* ongoing organizational health. An MBO with outside involvement is your second choice. An external sale is your third choice.

- Get legal and tax advisors involved *after* you've decided what you want to accomplish.

Succession Plan steps:

1. Establish your *exit goals*, *time frame*, and *what you want to do after you exit*.

2. Every year, re-establish the value of the company. Use a formula of 2½ to 4 times annualized pre-tax cash flow, from the perspective of an absentee-owner buyer. In some cases, specific hard assets, at current value, can be added. That formula most closely approximates true market value.

3. Carefully identify key staff—whose values fit the culture, who are good relationship-builders, and who are strong performers. Grade them on those specific points. Groom them for leadership by including them in the accountability for new business development, staff development, process improvement, and financial results.

4. Conversely, there are people in your company who aren't going to cut it. Improve the process of identifying them and firing them.

5. Identify likely future owners/buyers of the business, from all sources, and determine what would make the business more attractive to them.

6. Every year, evaluate your improvement in the five keys to business value:

   - *Consistent* profitability.

   - Healthy culture; loyal people; loyal customer base.

   - Good operating processes in place.

   - Business operations that are less dependent on current owners.

   - Financial accounting system that is accurate, timely, and meaningful.

# Product/Service Delivery

Look at your organization the way external customers see it. In their eyes, you exist to accomplish one thing—a product/service mix delivered to them. Because the external customer base sustains the organization, they're right: the essence of your business is the *consistent* quality of the product/service mix they receive. And that consistent quality depends on consistent execution of a well-managed delivery process.

The most effective mindset for process design is to think of the organization as a franchise—a business you will replicate. At the core of every franchise is their version of an operating manual, describing processes—actual steps and checklists—for *everything* the franchise does. Just like a franchisor, create your "operating manual" as if someone else could deliver your product/service mix simply by following the manual.

Product/service delivery process design:

1. Start with the external customer viewpoint. List exactly what the external customer receives.

2.  Working backward, look at each task that's done to produce those deliverables, and fit the tasks into *processes*.

3.  Design each process with a clean beginning, steps, times, accountable people, and ending with a finished product or service.

# Financial Reporting

A racecar driver doesn't need to be a mechanic. But because the driver's efforts are meaningless without a healthy car, a driver needs to know the indicators their mechanic measures, and what that tells them about the car's capabilities and performance.

The same principle applies in organizations. Leadership effectiveness depends on leaders receiving the right measures of capabilities and performance, most of which come through the financial reporting process.

A C.E.O. doesn't need to be an accountant, but does need to know how the accounting process measures and reports, so they can work with their accountant to get what they need: *meaningful, accurate, timely* information.

Relative to financial reporting, C.E.O.s need a working knowledge of four areas:

• *Basics of accounting*, and how that applies to planning, tracking, and reporting.

• *Balance Sheet* and *Income Statement*, the two most basic financial reports.

- *Cash Flow* projection and tracking.

- *Scorecards and Critical Numbers.*

# Basics of Accounting

Because accounting basics are simple and logical, this education will not take more than a session or two with an accountant. The payoff is knowledge you'll use constantly at the C.E.O. level. Here are five things you need to know:

1. *Chart of accounts.* This is the backbone of your financial reporting system. Learn how accounts are grouped (Assets, Liabilities, Equity, Revenue, Expenses) and how each account is used.

2. The processes by which information is posted to accounts. How do operating transactions become accounting entries? Does that process capture the transactions accurately? This is key to the *meaningfulness* of reports you receive.

3. How each account is reconciled. This shows you that the numbers you see are *accurate*.

4. How those account balances flow to specific financial reports.

5. The meaning of *accrual-basis* and *cash-basis* reporting, and the advantages of each.

# Balance Sheet and Income Statement

< *Income Statement* also known as
*Profit and Loss Statement*, or simply *P&L* >

These are the two basic financial reports that every
accounting system is programmed to produce, and every
lender is programmed to want. Together, these two
reports give a simple overview of the organization's
financial health.

Referring back to the chart of accounts: Asset, Liability, and Equity account balances flow to the *Balance
Sheet*. Revenue and Expense account balances flow to the
*Income Statement*. Both reports are produced only after
all accounts are reconciled at the end of a period (month,
year). The Balance Sheet shows the cumulative effect of
operations, and gives its picture only for the specific date
the period was closed. The Income Statement shows
operating results for an entire period.

# Cash Flow projection and tracking

While consistent profitability is the key indicator of organizational health, *cash* is its lifeblood. No matter how profitable you are, you cannot operate without cash, so you've got to have a process for projecting and tracking the actual cash that will flow in and out.

It's not easy. The key is *projecting*, and most accounting systems are not programmed to do it. Trained accountants can struggle with this, because they're taught debits and credits and balances, but the organization needs to project when its invoices will be paid, and when it will need to write checks.

The best examples are spreadsheets projecting ahead monthly for a year, listing all sources of cash receipts (receivables, deposits, draws, loans, other) and cash payments (payroll, payables, loan payments, bonuses, taxes, other), leading to a monthly net cash flow, and a projected month-end cash balance. With practice and diligence, it's a simple discipline to master.

# Scorecards and Critical Numbers

It *always* comes down to numbers. Plans require steps; steps produce outcomes; numbers measure outcomes.

Watch a professional sports event. The scoreboard gives an overview of the game, in numbers. Study the scoreboard for a minute, and you have a good picture—where each team stands in the game, and even what they need to do. If you could look at each coach's clipboard, you'd see more numbers, supporting the outcomes you see measured on the scoreboard.

And yet, most sports fans go to work in an organization where the "scoreboard" concept doesn't exist, they don't know where their team stands in the game, and they don't know what really needs to be done.

Effective C.E.O.s know that solutions come from everybody, and the best way to produce solutions is to involve the entire team, not just in the planning process, but in the measures, using some form of internal *scorecard* to communicate measured results to the team.

*Scorecards* are reports showing financial and other information in a format most meaningful to the organization using it. Generally, C.E.O.s choose an Income Statement format, with language and data appropriate to their game and their team.

*Critical numbers* are those few numbers that must move in the right direction in order to achieve organizational goals. Every plan has critical numbers—key measures on which the success of the plan depends. Those critical numbers are the simplest tools for communicating with your people, to keep them moving the organization forward. Critical numbers should be understood, tracked, communicated, and built into an incentive plan.

In discussions to determine critical numbers, everything is on the table. Revenue, gross margin, net profit, and cash are the obvious critical numbers. But every company has others: sales per desk, gross margin per producer, average ticket size, receivables, measures that truly drive your organizational health. For shorter-term goals, the numbers are even more proprietary: zero days lost to accidents, reduced percentage of scrap, fewer sales returns, ten new customers, whatever separate outcomes are required to reach your goals.

Critical numbers can be tracked at the individual level too. In professional services firms, utilization rates are a perfect example. Based on a company's critical numbers, individual numbers get people into the game by showing their contribution to company goals.

When the entire team knows the critical numbers, knows why they're important, and sees that they really do control the numbers, you have the forum to discuss what went right and what went wrong, and for people to create solutions.

# Business Development

The business development process has one goal: ongoing engagement of customers to pay for your services. Historically, the concept has been confusing, because the teaching focus has been on either marketing or selling, at the expense of the overall process.

That thinking has proven counter-productive. You can, for example, have the world's best marketing, but if your customer service is poor, your business development is doomed, and you'll never understand why, if your focus was on marketing. Clearly, it's a package deal:

*Business development is not about marketing, or even selling. It's about the entire process of establishing and maintaining relationships with people who will pay for the value you provide.*

Business development is based on three fundamentals:

- *Commit to the whole process.* Once you see how the steps fit together, it's a lot less complicated than most people believe. But the key is coordinating the entire process.

- *Continually improve your "inside reality"*—the quality of the product/service mix you deliver. That quality may not be visible to prospective customers. But in order to develop and retain business, it must be there. Your people must see it and *believe in it*.

- *Involve everyone.* The best solutions come from everyone. Keep them informed, and establish the expectation of their input and their shared ownership of results.

Business Development steps:

1. *Market Research.* The idea is to get your best customers to tell you how to get their attention, how to sell to them, and how to maintain that relationship. The challenge is that asking them specific questions—especially initially—tends to measure the wrong things. So the best market research is *your observation*, your conclusions, and then some customer questions. Here's what you need to determine:

   - Who are your best customers? Who *most values your service*, is willing and able to pay a fair price, and causes your people the fewest problems?

   - How did those customers *first* find out about you? Would there have been a better way? How *should* they have first found out about you?

- At the time their *initial* buying decision was made, why did they buy from you?

- What is the *one compelling reason* that keeps them as a customer?

2. *Position the Brand.* Brands are words or phrases that describe customer perception of the unique value of your product/service offer. Your brand exists whether or not you've been proactive creating it. Positioning is the process you follow to enable customers to find your brand, so they can buy it.

   Why is branding important? Because *customers*—all of us—think in terms of brands. Human nature gives customers narrow perceptions of product/service offers, and people show strong tendencies to base buying decisions, at least initially, on those perceptions.

   Buyers are attracted to *leadership*, by the way, so that's the strongest statement a brand can make. If you're not a category leader, narrow the category or create a new category where you can show leadership.

   Brand your *value*—the *outcome* to the customer. Volvo owns safety. Their brand is the outcome: the customer survives. You're not responsible for your customer's outcome, and your best customers understand that. But act as if you are, and deliver that message.

Positioning is all about differentiation. Based on what your market research tells you, determine the most effective process to communicate your brand, and enable customers to find you.

3. *Create sales.* Make sure your *sales process* is fully installed—that your sales force is trained in a structured process that works. Sales processes have four generic steps:

  • *Lead generation.* Market research conclusions will tell you the best way for initial contact with prospective customers.

  • *Needs analysis.* Here again, research is key. Understand the customer's challenges, and where your solutions fit. This is also the time to make a judgment call when there is not a fit. In other words, "If you take a beating in the beginning, it's only the beginning of the beating." Not everyone is a good prospective customer.

  • *Proposal/negotiation.* Most of the work in the sales process is done *before* this step. By this time, you should feel and act like you are already working with the customer.

- *Closing.* With the other steps done correctly, closing should seem like a natural conclusion.

Key to the success of the sales process is *managing* the process, and that begins with the compensation plan: you get the behavior you reward for. Make sure your compensation plan rewards sales success, and nothing else.

Sales people need to plan *goals* (daily, weekly, monthly, quarterly) that work for them *and* the organization. Sales managers use that planning process to coach accountability for numbers that sales people buy into.

4. *Close the back door.* With your best customers, your goal is to develop relationships that they will not want to end. These two selling fundamentals apply to existing customers:

First, it's a lot easier to maintain existing relationships than to develop new ones. It's easier because lead generation is done, and needs analysis is largely done. But maintaining those relationships still requires a process, goals, and follow-up.

Second, not every existing customer is a good one. Some don't value your service, some aren't willing to pay a fair price, some aren't able to pay, and some create problems. Those relationships need to be terminated. The loss of an unprofitable customer can be even more beneficial than gaining a profitable one. And the drama surrounding a bad customer relationship may well have a much larger negative impact than you were able to quantify.

# Human Resource Management

All process execution depends on people. Leaders with C.E.O. disciplines and skills, the right structure in place, and operating processes nailed down, still depend on the *right people*, performing at the right level.

> *Managing those human resources*
> *is leadership's greatest challenge.*

That challenge is met through sheer diligence, following four processes:

- Compensation Planning.

- Hiring and Firing.

- Performance Grading.

- Leadership Development.

## Compensation Planning

You get the behavior you reward for, so rule #1 in compensation planning is: put the carrot where you want the horse to go. The right people, paid by the hour, will show up. If paid to *do* something, they'll do it. When paid to do something *correctly*, they'll do it correctly.

Rule #2 is that the entire compensation process is about delivering messages: it's your single most important method of *communication* within the organization. People listen to what their paycheck says about the organization's values, it's goals, their role, and their value to the organization.

Compensation planning has three steps:

1. Because of the messages the plan delivers, it should be proprietary—created from scratch, and changed whenever you need to improve it. Start with your chart of positions. Using the position descriptions, estimate market pay range for each position. This is a simple process, but do your homework. There are no "salary surveys" that can shortcut this step, because there are no organizations whose industry, size, location and position descriptions are identical to yours. Gather market data from people you know or other

sources you trust. Then use *your judgment* to apply the data to your organization.

2. Knowing the market pay range for each position, decide where you want to be within the range. Healthy organizations stay in the upper half. (For positions paid by commission, base commissions on gross profit—not on sales, but on profitability of the sales—and pay on a cumulative year-to-date basis).

3. Some significant portion of your compensation plan should be an incentive for *organizational performance.* Many C.E.O.s believe that individual incentives are key, that group incentives condone individual non-performers. But experience and research clearly show that financial incentives *for the organization as a whole* are the bigger factor, and that individual under-performers will tend to step up or be weeded out by their peers. Determine organizational goals, and calculate a bonus pool for reaching goals.

# Hiring and Firing

"I never fired anybody too soon."

—C.E.O. Advisory Board comment

There were nine other C.E.O.s in the room when that comment was made, and every one of us understood its truth. We rarely regret letting go an under-performer, but we frequently regret not having done it sooner. As leaders, our job includes coaching people and believing in their ability. At the same time, some of our people are not "coachable", and the right thing to do is cut the cord quickly.

As critical as the hiring process is to organizational success, the firing process is *more* critical. That's because the hiring process is so inherently flawed that it can't be done consistently well. No matter how diligently you assess the attitudes and abilities of human beings, you will make mistakes. And once you've hired those mistakes, it's not wise to think they will acquire the attitudes and abilities you need, without hurting the organization while you wait. It's absolutely critical that you stick to your review process, and terminate people who don't measure up. Remember that championship Poker players aren't the ones who draw all aces. They're the ones who fold their bad hands early, so they have money to stay in the game.

Accept no compromise on hiring and retaining the best people for each position. If that means a position stays open longer, keep it open. If that means market wages have gone up, raise wages. The single greatest driver of your organizational success is the quality of your people. Hire and fire accordingly.

The hiring process begins with six questions we answer internally:

1. Why do we need this position filled?

2. In line with our goals, this position has what goals, and what responsibilities?

3. Which numbers define success in this position?

4. What compensation plan fits this position?

5. When will this position be graded?

6. What is the profile of the person who fits this position?

Knowing our answers, here are a dozen time-tested questions for candidates:

1. "Tell us your story—where you were born, where you grew up—right up through today. Take a few minutes, the floor is yours." This is a great first question. It starts the interview by putting the candidate in the role of doing the talking. And it tells us interesting things we'd probably not think to ask.

2. "Why did you get into this line of work?" Are they choice or chance? This answer tells you how much thought they put into their own decision-making, which also tells you a lot about their motivation.

3. "What is there about this industry, this company, or this job, that energizes you—that would make you want to get out of bed and be here on Monday mornings?" This answer is an indicator for attitude and fit. Energized people perform better, and make better decisions. But they must bring a capability to be energized.

4. "Where you work now, or used to work, what are the *people* like—bosses, peers, support people?" With their answer, they're really describing *themselves*, their attitude, and their outlook.

5. "How do you know when you've done a good job?" This will tell you if the person is a self-starter, or needs a constant pat on the back.

6. "Tell us something you accomplished that you feel really good about." This will tell you whether the person likes to work with individuals, groups, or non-people activities. Also, if they answer in detail, they like detail; if they answer briefly, they aren't likely to be detail-oriented.

7. "How do you think your performance in this position should be graded?" This is another indicator for both attitude and fit. The best performers want to improve, are comfortable being graded, and understand what's important and what's not.

8. "If it were up to you, how would you schedule a typical day or week in this position: commute time, arrival time, work time, departure time, work time after hours." This is a key to their work ethic.

9. "How do you stay organized?" Most any method is fine, as long as there's a method, not based on memory. During the interviews, do they take notes?

10. The best indicator of future performance is past performance, so include questions that let the applicant demonstrate specific expertise for the position; i.e., ask a controller the steps in their monthly close; ask a CSR to describe situations where they've resolved customer problems.

11. "Based on your perception of trends which could affect our industry, what are your thoughts on keeping a business like ours healthy?" Do they really see what's going on around them? Do they see the bigger picture? Do they think in terms of solutions?

12. "What do you like to do outside of work?" Do they make healthy choices?

When you close with, "Do you have any questions at all?" note the scope of what they ask. Their questions are indicators of professionalism, preparation, and critical thinking. In your assessment of the candidate, *always* follow your gut feeling.

# Performance Grading

Nothing in leadership is any more important than *consistent performance grading*, because that process delivers to our people four critical messages:

- We're in the people business, so your fit and your growth are our focus.

- Our culture is based 100% on core values and performance—both together, not one without the other—and you will be graded on both.

- Our organizational success depends on you, so we measure your effectiveness. We want you to know the measures, and know where you stand.

- We treat everyone honestly, and fairly. But we don't treat everyone equally. Our most effective leaders, our best performers, and our most creative people get the best rewards.

Grading is based on *numbers*, because effective leaders hold themselves and their people accountable to numbers. Front-end that process with mutual commitment on standards, goals, results, and consequences.

Reviews are not the place for kindness at the expense of accuracy—they must be brutally honest. For good people to do their best work, or for under-performers to leave, they need to know where they stand.

The key to the grading/review process is *follow-up*. Formal reviews must be *routine* (at least annually, possibly quarterly), and *sequential*, with each review setting the stage for the next one, and compensation plans tied to the review process.

People need to know up-front that excellent performance and ownership behavior bring the best rewards. Then they need to see it happen.

# Leadership Development

A good analogy for leadership development is the research that's been done on migratory geese. With a lot more experience than human C.E.O.s, migratory geese have demonstrated organizational success twice every year. They've learned:

- It's all about *leadership development*. Everyone they hire (A) *wants* to make the trip, and (B) can provide leadership along the way.

- Total focus is big picture: *mission accomplishment*. That's the glue that holds the team together.

- *All information is shared*. Everyone knows where the organization is headed. Everyone knows what it takes to get there.

- *Each individual needs the organization*. Because of the aerodynamic efficiency of formation flying, coupled with the hazards of air travel, each one knows they have virtually no chance of a successful migration alone.

- *Succession planning* is part of the culture. In their organization, the toughest job is the designated leadership position—"point bird" in the "V" formation. The demands of that position ensure organizational failure if only one bird could do the job. So when the leader tires and rotates to the end of the "V", the #2 bird takes the lead. Smooth transition.

Migratory geese understand leadership development, and get it done through their own processes of hiring, coaching, and firing. With human organizations, the concept is identical. In hiring, make sure candidates know where this train is headed—organizational values and goals—and *want to be on board.* Once they're on board, retain the ones whose reviews show their attitudes and efforts are providing leadership to the organization.

There are six coaching steps in a leadership development process:

1. *Educate* your people in the processes of running a healthy business. Share information that will show them how processes generate profit. Reward them for improving the processes. The right people, who are shown the correlation between their performance and organizational success, who are encouraged and incentivised to expand their roles and make improve-

ments, who are trusted to act like entrepreneurs, will get it done.

As they get it done, you'll see your best candidates for leadership development—those who are doing more, and getting others to do more, to move the organization forward.

2. Your best people will all be different. *Get to know them as individuals.* The most important key to employee retention is the relationship with their immediate supervisor. Own that relationship, and grow it.

   At the same time, remember that even among your best people, not everyone has leadership potential. Individuals have unique strengths and weaknesses. Don't expect people to overcome weaknesses. *Look for strengths*—primarily in C.E.O. disciplines and skills—and help them build those strengths.

3. *Keep ownership of work at the lowest level.* Let people know they own responsibility for results, and train them accordingly. Don't be "the boss with the answers". When people bring you a problem, ask them for a solution.

   Always assess yourself: *Is this working?* Is my coaching creating leaders, or dependents?

4. Use *coaching techniques* to improve individual solution ownership. Make sure people understand *why* something has to be done. Identify potential resources and solutions by asking questions. Educate people with examples of what has worked for others. In discussions about performance standards, use the customer's point of view, not your own. Let people tell you what they can accomplish, then give a reason to raise the bar, and have them figure out how to do it. Ask people what they need, then ask how they can get it. Always focus on improvement.

5. *Create a learning culture.* The greatest change in leadership qualifications over the last two generations is the requirement for *continuous learning*, simply because the pace of change is so much quicker. Force yourself and the people you coach (and the people they coach) to "get out more", to learn from exposure to others—peers, customers, vendors—even seminars and books. Create the forum internally for people to share what they learn, and push each other to improve.

6. *Make the position chart work.* Fundamental accountability is built in to the reporting requirements of that chart. People in senior leadership positions own the responsibility not only for their numbers, but

also for developing leaders in their part of the organization.

Throughout the organization, ensure that decision-making is done by individual leaders, in a *consultative* process, never a consensus process. (In consensus, a majority must agree. "Decision by committee" is inefficient at best, and also eliminates the key—*accountability*—that leaders need to learn to live with.) Coach your leaders to use a consultative process, where their people have input, but the leader keeps responsibility for the decision.

Done *consistently*, these six steps ensure one of three outcomes for developing leaders: (1) they learn to act successfully and stay on that path, (2) they accept responsibility for their failures and make corrections, or (3) they cannot (or will not) accept responsibility, and must be terminated. Either way, the well-prepared C.E.O. simply facilitates the process.

# *Execution*

It's been a hundred years since a research economist in England concluded that 80% of the wealth belonged to just 20% of the people. Expanding his research, he found the pattern to be some sort of natural law: in businesses, 80% of work was done by 20% of the people; 80% of profit came from 20% of sales. The math wasn't precise—"80/20" in any given situation might really be 70/30, 90/10, 99/1—the point being that a *majority of results* was always produced by a *minority of effort*.

In leadership, execution is so often stymied by the leader's own chosen distractions. So a lesson from the checklists is to look for "80/20" analogies in the way you spend your time. Knowing that 80% of your most productive work comes from 20% of your effort, reduce distractions and give yourself more productive time. Concurrently, identify the non-work activities that produce 80% of your happiness, and focus your free time there. You know the core relationships that sustain you, so spend more time with those people, and less time with everybody else.

> "We're lucky to play at this level."
>
> —C.E.O. Advisory Board comment

No matter what combination of discipline, skill, creativity, or bold decisions got us to the C.E.O. level, we're lucky to be here. How long we stay will depend on our *execution*.

The stumbling blocks to execution come primarily from failures within Checklist #1: leaders who don't have or don't use the disciplines and skills to play at this level. So the greatest lesson in this book is to live by Checklist #1. Those disciplines and skills enable you to execute the other checklists.

Never forget the simplicity of your leadership role. When it starts to feel complicated, that's nature's way of telling you there's a breakdown somewhere within the checklists—your disciplines, or structure, or processes. Deal with it, and *execute* the adjustments.

In any leadership role, the real qualification is *results*, so the key to execution is always asking objectively: "*Is this working?* What improvements are needed *today?*" The three C.E.O. checklists should keep you on that path.

Thankfully, Monday is coming again soon. In leadership, more than in any other role, Monday is a huge opportunity to get an entire week started on the right foot. So take control—*execute*—and enjoy the process.

978-0-595-47153-9
0-595-47153-6

www.ingramcontent.com/pod-product-compliance
Lightning Source LLC
Chambersburg PA
CBHW021544200526
45163CB00015B/1504